Penguins

by Alan Wood

 HOUGHTON MIFFLIN HARCOURT
School Publishers

PHOTOGRAPHY CREDITS: Cover © Hans Reinhard/zefa/Corbis. 1 © Arthur Morris/Corbis. 2 © age fotostock/CORBIS. 3 © Juan Carlos MuÒoz. 4 © Hans Reinhard/zefa/Corbis. 6 © Arthur Morris/Corbis. 7 Doug Allan/npl/Minden Pictures. 8 Konrad Wothe/Minden Pictures. 9 © Deddeda/Age Fotostock.

Printed in Hong Kong

ISBN-13: 978-0-547-02684-8
ISBN-10: 0-547-02684-6

2 3 4 5 6 7 8 0940 18 17 16 15 14 13 12 11 10

Table of Contents

All Kinds of Penguins

Many penguins live around
the world.
Some penguins are big,
and some are small.
Some have tall feathers on their
heads, and some do not.

Rockhopper penguin

All penguins have short legs.
They have webbed feet, too.
They do not have wings,
but they do have long flippers.
All penguins can sing.
They can also walk, jump, and slide,
but they cannot fly.

Sliding

Most penguins live near oceans.
They are great swimmers.
They use their feet to steer
through the water,
and they catch fish to eat.
Penguins have special feathers
that keep them dry.

Red areas show where penguins live.

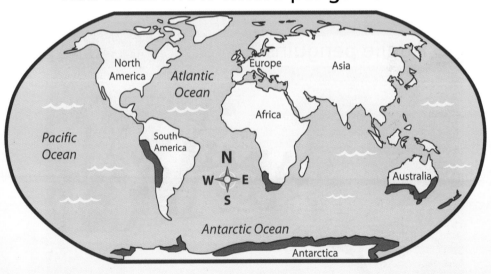

Penguins in Cold Places

Most penguins live in cold places.
Adélie penguins live in Antarctica.
They make their homes on the ice.
They have a thick layer of feathers
that helps them stay warm.
Rockhopper penguins live on
chilly beaches in South America.

Adélie penguins

Emperor penguins live
in Antarctica, too.
They are the biggest of
all the penguins.
Their big bodies can stay warm
in the cold.
Even junior Emperor penguins
are larger than many other birds.

Emperor penguins

Penguins in Warm Places

Other penguins live in warm places.

Fairy penguins live in Australia.

They are the smallest penguins.

They have tiny bodies.

They are also called

Little Blue penguins.

Fairy penguins

Some penguins live on sunny beaches. They do not have to worry about the cold. Sometimes they get too hot! They can stay in the water to keep cool.

Cormorants

Penguins of the World

For a long time, people weren't
sure how many kinds of penguins
there are.
Scientists finally agreed that
there are 17 kinds of penguins.
Find the penguins from this book
on the chart.

Name	Warm or Cold Place?
Adélie penguins	cold
Emperor penguins	cold
Fairy penguins	warm
Galapagos penguins	warm
Rockhopper penguins	cold

Responding

✔ **TARGET SKILL** **Main Ideas and Details**

What is the main idea of this book?
Copy this chart. Write one detail about
the main idea.

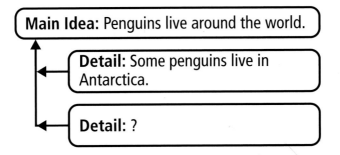

Main Idea: Penguins live around the world.

Detail: Some penguins live in Antarctica.

Detail: ?

✏ Write About It

Text to World Some penguins live in zoos.
Zookeepers must make the penguins
comfortable. Pick a penguin from this
book. Write a paragraph to explain how a
zookeeper should set up its new home.

finally	steer
junior	waterproof
otherwise	webbed
slippery	whistle

✔ **TARGET SKILL** **Main Ideas and Details** Tell important ideas and details about a topic.

✔ **TARGET STRATEGY** **Infer/Predict** Use text clues to figure out important ideas.

GENRE **Narrative nonfiction** tells a true story about a topic.